I0412140

Second State of the Union Address

JAMES BUCHANAN

Published in 1858

TABLE OF CONTENTS

SECOND STATE OF THE UNION ADDRESS

SECOND STATE OF THE UNION ADDRESS

Fellow-Citizens of the Senate and House of Representatives:

When we compare the condition of the country at the present day with what it was one year ago at the meeting of Congress, we have much reason for gratitude to that Almighty Providence which has never failed to interpose for our relief at the most critical periods of our history. One year ago the sectional strife between the North and the South on the dangerous subject of slavery had again become so intense as to threaten the peace and perpetuity of the Confederacy. The application for the admission of Kansas as a State into the Union fostered this unhappy agitation and brought the whole subject once more before Congress. It was the desire of every patriot that such measures of legislation might be adopted as would remove the excitement from the States and confine it to the Territory where it legitimately belonged. Much has been done, I am happy to say, toward the accomplishment of this object during the last session of Congress. The Supreme Court of the United States had previously decided that all American citizens have an equal right to take into the Territories whatever is held as property under the laws of any of the States, and to hold such property there under the guardianship of the Federal Constitution so long as the Territorial condition shall remain.

This is now a well-established position, and the proceedings of the last session were alone wanting to give it practical effect. The principle has been recognized in some form or other by an almost unanimous vote of both Houses of Congress that a Territory has a right to come into the Union either as a free or a slave State, according to the will of a majority of its people. The just equality of all the States has thus been vindicated and a fruitful source of dangerous dissension among them has been removed.

Whilst such has been the beneficial tendency of your legislative proceedings outside of Kansas, their influence has nowhere been so happy as within that Territory itself. Left to manage and control its own affairs in its own way, without the pressure of external influence, the revolutionary Topeka organization and all resistance to the Territorial government established by Congress have been finally abandoned. As a natural consequence that fine Territory now appears to be tranquil and prosperous and is attracting increasing thousands of immigrants to make it their happy home.

The past unfortunate experience of Kansas has enforced the lesson, so often already taught, that resistance to lawful authority under our form of government can not fail in the end to prove disastrous to its authors. Had the people of the Territory yielded obedience to the laws enacted by their legislature, it would at the present moment have contained a large additional population of industrious and enterprising citizens, who have been deterred from entering its borders by the existence of civil strife and organized rebellion.

It was the resistance to rightful authority and the persevering attempts to establish a revolutionary government under the Topeka constitution which caused the people of Kansas to commit the grave error of refusing to vote for delegates to the convention to frame a constitution under a law not denied to be fair and just in its provisions. This refusal to vote has been the prolific source of all the evils which have followed, In their hostility to the Territorial government they disregarded the principle, absolutely essential to the working of our form of government, that a majority of those who vote, not the majority who may remain at home, from whatever cause, must decide the result of an election. For this reason, seeking to take advantage of their own error, they denied the authority of the convention thus elected to frame a constitution.

The convention, notwithstanding, proceeded to adopt a constitution unexceptionable in its general features, and providing for the submission of the slavery question to a vote of the people, which, in my opinion, they were bound to do under the Kansas and Nebraska act. This was the all-important question which had alone convulsed the Territory; and yet the opponents of the lawful government, persisting in their first error, refrained from exercising their right to vote, and preferred that slavery should continue rather than surrender their revolutionary Topeka organization.

A wiser and better spirit seemed to prevail before the first Monday of January last, when an election was held under the constitution. A majority of the people then voted for a governor and other State officers, for a Member of Congress and members of the State legislature. This election was warmly contested by the two political parties in Kansas, and a greater vote was polled than at any previous election. A large majority of the members of the legislature elect belonged to that party which had previously refused to vote. The antislavery party were thus placed in the ascendant, and the political power of the State was in their own hands. Had Congress admitted Kansas into the Union under the Lecompton constitution, the legislature might at its very first session have submitted the question to a vote of the people whether they would or would not have a convention to amend their constitution, either on the slavery or any other question, and have adopted all necessary means for giving speedy effect to the will of the majority. Thus the Kansas question would have been immediately and finally settled.

Under these circumstances I submitted to Congress the constitution thus framed, with all the officers already elected necessary to put the State government into operation, accompanied by a strong recommendation in favor of the admission of Kansas as a State. In the course of my long public life I have never performed any official act which in the retrospect has afforded me more heartfelt satisfaction. Its admission could have inflicted no possible injury on any human being, whilst it would within a brief period have restored peace to Kansas and harmony to the Union. In that event the slavery question would ere this have been finally settled according to the legally expressed will of a majority of the voters, and popular sovereignty would thus have been vindicated in a constitutional manner.

With my deep convictions of duty I could have pursued no other course. It is true that as an individual I had expressed an opinion, both before and during the session of the convention, in favor of submitting the remaining clauses of the constitution, as well as that concerning slavery, to the people. But, acting in an official character, neither myself nor any human authority had the power to rejudge the proceedings of the convention and declare the constitution which it had framed to be a nullity. To have done this would have been a violation of the Kansas and Nebraska act, which left the people of the Territory "perfectly free to form and regulate their domestic institutions in their own way, subject only to the Constitution of the United States." It would equally have violated the great principle of popular sovereignty, at the foundation of our institutions, to deprive the people of the power, if they thought proper to exercise it, of confiding to delegates elected by themselves the trust of framing a constitution without requiring them to subject their constituents to the trouble, expense, and delay of a second election. It would have been in opposition to many precedents in our history, commencing in the very best age of the Republic, of the admission of Territories as States into the Union without a previous vote of the people approving their constitution.

It is to be lamented that a question so insignificant when viewed in its practical effects on the people of Kansas, whether decided one way or the other, should have kindled such a flame of excitement throughout the country. This reflection may prove to be a lesson of wisdom and of warning for our future guidance. Practically considered, the question is simply whether the people of that Territory should first come into the Union and then change any provision in their constitution not agreeable to themselves, or accomplish the very same object by remaining out of the Union and framing another constitution in accordance with their will. In either case the result would be precisely the same. The only difference, in point of fact, is that the object would have been much sooner attained and the pacification of Kansas more speedily effected had it been admitted as a State during the last session of Congress.

My recommendation, however, for the immediate admission of Kansas failed to meet the approbation of Congress. They deemed it wiser to adopt a different measure for the settlement of the question. For my own part, I should have been willing to yield my assent to almost any constitutional measure to accomplish this object. I therefore cordially acquiesced in what has been called the English compromise and approved the "act for the admission of the State of Kansas into the Union" upon the terms therein prescribed.

Under the ordinance which accompanied the Lecompton constitution the people of Kansas had claimed double the quantity of public lands for the support of common schools which had ever been previously granted to any State upon entering the Union, and also the alternate sections of land for 12 miles on each side of two railroads proposed to be constructed from the northern to the southern boundary and from the eastern to the western boundary of the State. Congress, deeming these claims unreasonable, provided by the act of May 4, 1858, to which I have just referred, for the admission of the State on an equal footing with the original States, but "upon the fundamental condition precedent" that a majority of the people thereof, at an election to be held for that purpose, should, in place of the very large grants of public lands which they had demanded under the ordinance, accept such grants as had been made to Minnesota and other new States. Under this act, should a majority reject the proposition offered them, "it shall be deemed and held that the people of Kansas do not desire admission into the Union with said constitution under the conditions set forth in said proposition." In that event the act authorizes the people of the Territory to elect delegates to form a constitution and State government for themselves "whenever, and not before, it is ascertained by a census, duly and legally taken, that the population of said Territory equals or exceeds the ratio of representation required for a member of the House of Representatives of the Congress of the United States." The delegates thus assembled "shall first determine by a vote whether it is the wish of the people of the proposed State to be admitted into the Union at that time, and, if so, shall proceed to form a constitution and take all necessary steps for the establishment of a State government in conformity with the Federal Constitution." After this constitution shall have been formed, Congress, carrying out the principles of popular sovereignty and nonintervention, have left "the mode and manner of its approval or ratification by the people of the proposed State" to be "prescribed by law," and they "shall then be admitted into the Union as a State under such constitution, thus fairly and legally made, with or without slavery, as said constitution may prescribe."

An election was held throughout Kansas, in pursuance of the provisions of this act, on the 2d day of August last, and it resulted in the rejection by a large majority of the proposition submitted to the people by Congress. This being the case, they are now authorized to form another constitution, preparatory to admission into the Union, but not until their number, as ascertained by a census, shall equal or exceed the ratio required to elect a member to the House of Representatives.

It is not probable, in the present state of the case, that a third constitution can be lawfully framed and presented to Congress by Kansas before its population shall have reached the designated number. Nor is it to be presumed that after their sad experience in resisting the Territorial laws they will attempt to adopt a constitution in express violation of the provisions of an act of Congress. During the session of 1856 much of the time of Congress was occupied on the question of admitting Kansas under the Topeka constitution. Again, nearly the whole of the last session was devoted to the question of its admission under the Lecompton constitution. Surely it is not unreasonable to require the people of Kansas to wait before making a third attempt until the number of their inhabitants shall amount to 93,420. During this brief period the harmony of the States as well as the great business interests of the country demand that the people of the Union shall not for a third time be convulsed by another agitation on the Kansas question. By waiting for a short time and acting in obedience to law Kansas will glide into the Union without the slightest impediment.

This excellent provision, which Congress have applied to Kansas, ought to be extended and rendered applicable to all Territories which may hereafter seek admission into the Union.

Whilst Congress possess the undoubted power of admitting a new State into the Union, however small may be the number of its inhabitants, yet this power ought not, in my opinion, to be exercised before the population shall amount to the ratio required by the act for the admission of Kansas. Had this been previously the rule, the country would have escaped all the evils and misfortunes to which it has been exposed by the Kansas question.

Of course it would be unjust to give this rule a retrospective application, and exclude a State which, acting upon the past practice of the Government, has already formed its constitution, elected its legislature and other officers, and is now prepared to enter the Union. The rule ought to be adopted, whether we consider its bearing on the people of the Territories or upon the people of the existing States. Many of the serious dissentions which have prevailed in Congress and throughout the country would have been avoided had this rule been established at an earlier period of the Government.

Immediately upon the formation of a new Territory people from different States and from foreign countries rush into it for the laudable purpose of improving their condition. Their first duty to themselves is to open and cultivate farms, to construct roads, to establish schools, to erect places of religious worship, and to devote their energies generally to reclaim the wilderness and to lay the foundations of a flourishing and prosperous commonwealth. If in this incipient condition, with a population of a few thousand, they should prematurely enter the Union, they are oppressed by the burden of State taxation, and the means necessary for the improvement of the Territory and the advancement of their own interests are thus diverted to very different purposes.

The Federal Government has ever been a liberal parent to the Territories and a generous contributor to the useful enterprises of the early settlers. It has paid the expenses of their governments and legislative assemblies out of the common Treasury, and thus relieved them from a heavy charge. Under these circumstances nothing can be better calculated to retard their material progress than to divert them from their useful employments by prematurely exciting angry political contests among themselves for the benefit of aspiring leaders. It is surely no hardship for embryo governors, Senators, and Members of Congress to wait until the number of inhabitants shall equal those of a single Congressional district. They surely ought not to be permitted to rush into the Union with a population less than one-half of several of the large counties in the interior of some of the States. This was the condition of Kansas when it made application to be admitted under the Topeka constitution. Besides, it requires some time to render the mass of a population collected in a new Territory at all homogeneous and to unite them on anything like a fixed policy. Establish the rule, and all will look forward to it and govern themselves accordingly. But justice to the people of the several States requires that this rule should be established by Congress. Each State is entitled to two Senators and at least one Representative in Congress. Should the people of the States fail to elect a Vice-President, the power devolves upon the Senate to select this officer from the two highest candidates on the list. In case of the death of the President, the Vice-President thus elected by the Senate becomes President of the United States. On all questions of legislation the Senators from the smallest States of the Union have an equal vote with those from the largest. The same may be said in regard to the ratification of treaties and of

Executive appointments. All this has worked admirably in practice, whilst it conforms in principle with the character of a Government instituted by sovereign States. I presume no American citizen would desire the slightest change in the arrangement. Still, is it not unjust and unequal to the existing States to invest some 40,000 or 50,000 people collected in a Territory with the attributes of sovereignty and place them on an equal footing with Virginia and New York in the Senate of the United States?

For these reasons I earnestly recommend the passage of a general act which shall provide that, upon the application of a Territorial legislature declaring their belief that the Territory contains a number of inhabitants which, if in a State, would entitle them to elect a Member of Congress, it shall be the duty of the President to cause a census of the inhabitants to be taken, and if found sufficient then by the terms of this act to authorize them to proceed "in their own way" to frame a State constitution preparatory to admission into the Union. I also recommend that an appropriation may be made to enable the President to take a census of the people of Kansas.

The present condition of the Territory of Utah, when contrasted with what it was one year ago, is a subject for congratulation. It was then in a state of open rebellion, and, cost what it might, the character of the Government required that this rebellion should be suppressed and the Mormons compelled to yield obedience to the Constitution and the laws. In order to accomplish this object, as I informed you in my last annual message, I appointed a new governor instead of Brigham Young, and other Federal officers to take the place of those who, consulting their personal safety, had found it necessary to withdraw from the Territory.

To protect these civil officers, and to aid them, as a posse comitatus, in the execution of the laws in case of need, I ordered a detachment of the Army to accompany them to Utah. The necessity for adopting these measures is now demonstrated.

On the 15th of September, 1857, Governor Young issued his proclamation, in the style of an independent sovereign, announcing his purpose to resist by force of arms the entry of the United States troops into our own Territory of Utah. By this he required all the forces in the Territory to "hold themselves in readiness to march at a moment's notice to repel any and all such invasion," and established martial law from its date throughout the Territory. These proved to be no idle threats. Forts Bridger and Supply were vacated and burnt down by the Mormons to deprive our troops of a shelter after their long and fatiguing march. Orders were issued by Daniel H. Wells, styling himself "Lieutenant General, Nauvoo Legion," to stampede the animals of the United States troops on their march, to set fire to their trains, to burn the grass and the whole country before them and on their flanks, to keep them from sleeping by night surprises, and to blockade the road by felling trees and destroying the fords of rivers, etc.

These orders were promptly and effectually obeyed. On the 4th of October, 1857, the Mormons captured and burned, on Green River, three of our supply trains, consisting of seventy-five wagons loaded with provisions and tents for the army, and carried away several hundred animals. This diminished the supply of provisions so materially that General Johnston was obliged to reduce the ration, and even with this precaution there was only sufficient left to subsist the troops until the 1st of June.

Our little army behaved admirably in their encampment at Fort Bridger under these trying privations. In the midst of the mountains, in a dreary, unsettled, and inhospitable region, more than a thousand miles from home, they passed the severe and inclement winter without a murmur. They looked forward with confidence for relief from their country in due season, and in this they were not disappointed. The Secretary of War employed all his energies to forward them the necessary supplies and to muster and send such a military force to Utah as would render resistance on the part of the Mormons hopeless, and thus terminate the war without the effusion of blood. In his efforts he was efficiently sustained by Congress. They granted appropriations sufficient to cover the deficiency thus necessarily created, and also provided for raising two regiments of volunteers "for the purpose of quelling disturbances in the Territory of Utah, for the protection of supply and emigrant trains, and the suppression of Indian hostilities on the frontiers." Happily, there was no occasion to call these regiments into service. If there had been, I should have felt serious embarrassment in selecting them, so great was the number of our brave and patriotic citizens anxious to serve their country in this distant and apparently dangerous expedition. Thus it has ever been, and thus may it ever be.

The wisdom and economy of sending sufficient reenforcements to Utah are established, not only by the event, but in the opinion of those who from their position and opportunities are the most capable of forming a correct judgment. General Johnston, the commander of the forces, in addressing the Secretary of War from Fort Bridger under date of October 18, 1857, expresses the opinion that "unless a large force is sent here, from the nature of the country a protracted war on their [the Mormons's] part is inevitable." This he considered necessary to terminate the war "speedily and more economically than if attempted by insufficient means."

In the meantime it was my anxious desire that the Mormons should yield obedience to the Constitution and the laws without rendering it necessary to resort to military force. To aid in accomplishing this object, I deemed it advisable in April last to dispatch two distinguished citizens of the United States, Messrs. Powell and McCulloch, to Utah. They bore with them a proclamation addressed by myself to the inhabitants of Utah, dated on the 6th day of that month, warning them of their true condition and how hopeless it was on their part to persist in rebellion against the United States, and offering all those who should submit to the laws a full pardon for their past seditions and treasons. At the same time I assured those who should persist in rebellion against the United States that they must expect no further lenity, but look to be rigorously dealt with according to their deserts. The instructions to these agents, as well as a copy of the proclamation and their reports, are herewith submitted. It will be seen by their report of the 3d of July last that they have fully confirmed the opinion expressed by General Johnston in the previous October as to the necessity of sending reenforcements to Utah. In this they state that they "are firmly impressed with the belief that the presence of the Army here and the large additional force that had been ordered to this Territory were the chief inducements that caused the Mormons to abandon the idea of resisting the authority of the United States. A less decisive policy would probably have resulted in a long, bloody, and expensive war."

These gentlemen conducted themselves to my entire satisfaction and rendered useful services in executing the humane intentions of the Government.

It also affords me great satisfaction to state that Governor Cumming has performed his duty in an able and conciliatory manner and with the happiest effect. I can not in this connection refrain from mentioning the valuable services of Colonel Thomas L. Kane, who, from motives of pure benevolence and without any official character or pecuniary compensation, visited Utah during the last inclement winter for the purpose of contributing to the pacification of the Territory.

I am happy to inform you that the governor and other civil officers of Utah are now performing their appropriate functions without resistance. The authority of the Constitution and the laws has been fully restored and peace prevails throughout the Territory. A portion of the troops sent to Utah are now encamped in Cedar Valley, 44 miles southwest of Salt Lake City, and the remainder have been ordered to Oregon to suppress Indian hostilities.

The march of the army to Salt Lake City through the Indian Territory has had a powerful effect in restraining the hostile feelings against the United States which existed among the Indians in that region and in securing emigrants to the far West against their depredations. This will also be the means of establishing military posts and promoting settlements along the route. I recommend that the benefits of our land laws and preemption system be extended to the people of Utah by the establishment of a land office in that Territory.

I have occasion also to congratulate you on the result of our negotiations with China.

You were informed by my last annual message that our minister had been instructed to occupy a neutral position in the hostilities conducted by Great Britain and France against Canton. He was, however, at the same time directed to cooperate cordially with the British and French ministers in all peaceful measures to secure by treaty those just concessions to foreign commerce which the nations of the world had a right to demand. It was impossible for me to proceed further than this on my own authority without usurping the war-making power, which under the Constitution belongs exclusively to Congress.

Besides, after a careful examination of the nature and extent of our grievances, I did not believe they were of such a pressing and aggravated character as would have justified Congress in declaring war against the Chinese Empire without first making another earnest attempt to adjust them by peaceful negotiation. I was the more inclined to this opinion because of the severe chastisement which had then but recently been inflicted upon the Chinese by our squadron in the capture and destruction of the Barrier forts to avenge an alleged insult to our flag. The event has proved the wisdom of our neutrality. Our minister has executed his instructions with eminent skill and ability. In conjunction with the Russian plenipotentiary, he has peacefully, but effectually, cooperated with the English and French plenipotentiaries, and each of the four powers has concluded a separate treaty with China of a highly satisfactory character. The treaty concluded by our own plenipotentiary will immediately be submitted to the Senate.

I am happy to announce that through the energetic yet conciliatory efforts of our consul-general in Japan a new treaty has been concluded with that Empire, which may be expected materially to augment our trade and intercourse in that quarter and remove from our countrymen the disabilities which have heretofore been imposed upon the exercise of their religion. The treaty shall be submitted to the Senate for approval without delay.

It is my earnest desire that every misunderstanding with the Government of Great Britain should be amicably and speedily adjusted. It has been the misfortune of both countries, almost ever since the period of the Revolution, to have been annoyed by a succession of irritating and dangerous questions, threatening their friendly relations. This has partially prevented the full development of those feelings of mutual friendship between the people of the two countries so natural in themselves and so conducive to their common interest. Any serious interruption of the commerce between the United States and Great Britain would be equally injurious to both. In fact, no two nations have ever existed on the face of the earth which could do each other so much good or so much harm.

Entertaining these sentiments, I am gratified to inform you that the long-pending controversy between the two Governments in relation to the question of visitation and search has been amicably adjusted. The claim on the part of Great Britain forcibly to visit American vessels on the high seas in time of peace could not be sustained under the law of nations, and it had been overruled by her own most eminent jurists. This question was recently brought to an issue by the repeated acts of British cruisers in boarding and searching our merchant vessels in the Gulf of Mexico and the adjacent seas. These acts were the more injurious and annoying, as these waters are traversed by a large portion of the commerce and navigation of the United States and their free and unrestricted use is essential to the security of the coastwise trade between the different States of the Union. Such vexatious interruptions could not fail to excite the feelings of the country and to require the interposition of the Government. Remonstrances were addressed to the British Government against these violations of our rights of sovereignty, and a naval force was at the same time ordered to the Cuban waters with directions "to protect all vessels of the United States on the high seas from search or detention by the vessels of war of any other nation." These measures received the unqualified and even enthusiastic approbation of the American people. Most fortunately, however, no collision took place, and the British Government promptly avowed its recognition of the principles of international law upon this subject as laid down by the Government of the United States in the note of the Secretary of State to the British minister at Washington of April 10, 1858, which secure the vessels of the United States upon the high seas from visitation or search in time of peace under any circumstances whatever. The claim has been abandoned in a manner reflecting honor on the British Government and evincing a just regard for the law of nations, and can not fail to strengthen the amicable relations between the two countries.

The British Government at the same time proposed to the United States that some mode should be adopted, by mutual arrangement between the two countries, of a character which may be found effective without being offensive, for verifying the nationality of vessels suspected on good grounds of carrying false colors. They have also invited the United States to take the initiative and propose measures for this purpose. Whilst declining to assume so grave a responsibility, the Secretary of State has informed the British Government that we are ready to receive any proposals which they may feel disposed to offer having this object in view, and to consider them in an amicable spirit. A strong opinion is, however, expressed that the occasional abuse of the flag of any nation is an evil far less to be deprecated than would be the establishment of any regulations which might be incompatible with the freedom of the seas. This Government has yet received no communication specifying the manner in which the British Government would propose to carry out their suggestion, and I am inclined to believe that no plan which can be devised will be free from grave embarrassments. Still, I shall form no decided opinion on the subject until I shall have carefully and in the best spirit examined any proposals which they may think proper to make.

I am truly sorry I can not also inform you that the complications between Great Britain and the United States arising out of the Clayton and Bulwer treaty of April, 1850, have been finally adjusted.

At the commencement of your last session I had reason to hope that, emancipating themselves from further unavailing discussions, the two Governments would proceed to settle the Central American questions in a practical manner, alike honorable and satisfactory to both; and this hope I have not yet abandoned. In my last annual message I stated that overtures had been made by the British Government for this purpose in a friendly spirit, which I cordially reciprocated. Their proposal was to withdraw these questions from direct negotiation between the two Governments, but to accomplish the same object by a negotiation between the British Government and each of the Central American Republics whose territorial interests are immediately involved. The settlement was to be made in accordance with the general tenor of the interpretation placed upon the Clayton and Bulwer treaty by the United States, with certain modifications. As negotiations are still pending upon this basis, it would not be proper for me now to communicate their present condition. A final settlement of these questions is greatly to be desired, as this would wipe out the last remaining subject of dispute between the two countries.

Our relations with the great Empires of France and Russia, as well as with all other Governments on the continent of Europe, except that of Spain, continue to be of the most friendly character.

With Spain our relations remain in an unsatisfactory condition. In my message of December last I informed you that our envoy extraordinary and minister plenipotentiary to Madrid had asked for his recall, and it was my purpose to send out a new minister to that Court with special instructions on all questions pending between the two Governments, and with a determination to have them speedily and amicably adjusted if that were possible. This purpose has been hitherto defeated by causes which I need not enumerate. The mission to Spain has been intrusted to a distinguished citizen of Kentucky, who will proceed to Madrid without delay and make another and a final attempt to obtain justice from that Government.

Spanish officials under the direct control of the Captain-General of Cuba have insulted our national flag and in repeated instances have from time to time inflicted injuries on the persons and property of our citizens. These have given birth to numerous claims against the Spanish Government, the merits of which have been ably discussed for a series of years by our successive diplomatic representatives. Notwithstanding this, we have not arrived at a practical result in any single instance, unless we may except the case of the Black Warrior, under the late Administration, and that presented an outrage of such a character as would have justified an immediate resort to war. All our attempts to obtain redress have been baffled and defeated.

The frequent and oft-recurring changes in the Spanish ministry have been employed as reasons for delay. We have been compelled to wait again and again until the new minister shall have had time to investigate the justice of our demands.

Even what have been denominated "the Cuban claims," in which more than 100 of our citizens are directly interested, have furnished no exception. These claims were for the refunding of duties unjustly exacted from American vessels at different custom-houses in Cuba so long ago as the year 1844. The principles upon which they rest are so manifestly equitable and just that, after a period of nearly ten years, in 1854 they were recognized by the Spanish Government. Proceedings were afterwards instituted to ascertain their amount, and this was finally fixed, according to their own statement (with which we were satisfied), at the sum of $128,635.54. Just at the moment, after a delay of fourteen years, when we had reason to expect that this sum would be repaid with interest, we have received a proposal offering to refund one-third of that amount ($42,878.41), but without interest, if we would accept this in full satisfaction. The offer is also accompanied by a declaration that this indemnification is not founded on any reason of strict justice, but is made as a special favor.

One alleged cause for procrastination in the examination and adjustment of our claims arises from an obstacle which it is the duty of the Spanish Government to remove. Whilst the Captain-General of Cuba is invested with general despotic authority in the government of that island, the power is withheld from him to examine and redress wrongs committed by officials under his control on citizens of the United States. Instead of making our complaints directly to him at Havana, we are obliged to present them through our minister at Madrid. These are then referred back to the Captain-General for information, and much time is thus consumed in preliminary investigations and correspondence between Madrid and Cuba before the Spanish Government will consent to proceed to negotiation. Many of the difficulties between the two Governments would be obviated and a long train of negotiation avoided if the Captain-General were invested with authority to settle questions of easy solution on the spot, where all the facts are fresh and could be promptly and satisfactorily ascertained. We have hitherto in vain urged upon the Spanish Government to confer this power upon the Captain-General, and our minister to Spain will again be instructed to urge this subject on their notice. In this respect we occupy a different position from the powers of Europe. Cuba is almost within sight of our shores; our commerce with it is far greater than that of any other nation, including Spain itself, and our citizens are in habits of daily and extended personal intercourse with every part of the island. It is therefore a great grievance that when any difficulty occurs, no matter how unimportant, which might be readily settled at the moment, we should be obliged to resort to Madrid, especially when the very first step to be taken there is to refer it back to Cuba.

The truth is that Cuba, in its existing colonial condition, is a constant source of injury and annoyance to the American people. It is the only spot in the civilized world where the African slave trade is tolerated, and we are bound by treaty with Great Britain to maintain a naval force on the coast of Africa, at much expense both of life and treasure, solely for the purpose of arresting slavers bound to that island. The late serious difficulties between the United States and Great Britain respecting the right of search, now so happily terminated, could never have arisen if Cuba had not afforded a market for slaves. As long as this market shall remain open there can be no hope for the civilization of benighted Africa. Whilst the demand for slaves continues in Cuba wars will be waged among the petty and barbarous chiefs in Africa for the purpose of seizing subjects to supply this trade. In such a condition of affairs it is impossible that the light of civilization and religion can ever penetrate these dark abodes.

It has been made known to the world by my predecessors that the United States have on several occasions endeavored to acquire Cuba from Spain by honorable negotiation. If this were accomplished, the last relic of the African slave trade would instantly disappear. We would not, if we could, acquire Cuba in any other manner. This is due to our national character. All the territory which we have acquired since the origin of the Government has been by fair purchase from France, Spain, and Mexico or by the free and voluntary act of the independent State of Texas in blending her destinies with our own. This course we shall ever pursue, unless circumstances should occur which we do not now anticipate, rendering a departure from it clearly justifiable under the imperative and overruling law of self-preservation. The island of Cuba, from its geographical position, commands the mouth of the Mississippi and the immense and annually increasing trade, foreign and coastwise, from the valley of that noble river, now embracing half the sovereign States of the Union. With that island under the dominion of a distant foreign power this trade, of vital importance to these States, is exposed to the danger of being destroyed in time of war, and it has hitherto been subjected to perpetual injury and annoyance in time of peace. Our relations with Spain, which ought to be of the most friendly character, must always be placed in jeopardy whilst the existing colonial government over the island shall remain in its present condition.

Whilst the possession of the island would be of vast importance to the United States, its value to Spain is comparatively unimportant. Such was the relative situation of the parties when the great Napoleon transferred Louisiana to the United States. Jealous as he ever was of the national honor and interests of France, no person throughout the world has imputed blame to him for accepting a pecuniary equivalent for this cession.

The publicity which has been given to our former negotiations upon this subject and the large appropriation which may be required to effect the purpose render it expedient before making another attempt to renew the negotiation that I should lay the whole subject before Congress. This is especially necessary, as it may become indispensable to success that I should be intrusted with the means of making an advance to the Spanish Government immediately after the signing of the treaty, without awaiting the ratification of it by the Senate. I am encouraged to make this suggestion by the example of Mr. Jefferson previous to the purchase of Louisiana from France and by that of Mr. Polk in view of the acquisition of territory from Mexico. I refer the whole subject to Congress and commend it to their careful consideration.

I repeat the recommendation made in my message of December last in favor of an appropriation "to be paid to the Spanish Government for the purpose of distribution among the claimants in the Amistad case." President Polk first made a similar recommendation in December, 1847, and it was repeated by my immediate predecessor in December, 1853. I entertain no doubt that indemnity is fairly due to these claimants under our treaty with Spain of October 27, 1795; and whilst demanding justice we ought to do justice. An appropriation promptly made for this purpose could not fail to exert a favorable influence on our negotiations with Spain.

Our position in relation to the independent States south of us on this continent, and especially those within the limits of North America, is of a peculiar character. The northern boundary of Mexico is coincident with our own southern boundary from ocean to ocean, and we must necessarily feel a deep interest in all that concerns the well-being and the fate of so near a neighbor. We have always cherished the kindest wishes for the success of that Republic, and have indulged the hope that it might at last, after all its trials, enjoy peace and prosperity under a free and stable government. We have never hitherto interfered, directly or indirectly, with its internal affairs, and it is a duty which we owe to ourselves to protect the integrity of its territory against the hostile interference of any other power. Our geographical position, our direct interest in all that concerns Mexico, and our well-settled policy in regard to the North American continent render this an indispensable duty.

Mexico has been in a state of constant revolution almost ever since it achieved its independence. One military leader after another has usurped the Government in rapid succession, and the various constitutions from time to time adopted have been set at naught almost as soon as they were proclaimed. The successive Governments have afforded no adequate protection, either to Mexican citizens or foreign residents, against lawless violence. Heretofore a seizure of the capital by a military chieftain has been generally followed by at least the nominal submission of the country to his rule for a brief period, but not so at the present crisis of Mexican affairs. A civil war has been raging for some time throughout the Republic between the central Government at the City of Mexico, which has endeavored to subvert the constitution last framed by military power, and those who maintain the authority of that constitution. The antagonist parties each hold possession of different States of the Republic, and the fortunes of the war are constantly changing. Meanwhile the most reprehensible means have been employed by both parties to extort money from foreigners, as well as natives, to carry on this ruinous contest. The truth is that this fine country, blessed with a productive soil and a benign climate, has been reduced by civil dissension to a condition of almost hopeless anarchy and imbecility. It would be vain for this Government to attempt to enforce payment in money of the claims of American citizens, now amounting to more than $10,000,000, against Mexico, because she is destitute of all pecuniary means to satisfy these demands.

Our late minister was furnished with ample powers and instructions for the adjustment of all pending questions with the central Government of Mexico, and he performed his duty with zeal and ability. The claims of our citizens, some of them arising out of the violation of an express provision of the treaty of Guadalupe Hidalgo, and others from gross injuries to persons as well as property, have remained unredressed and even unnoticed. Remonstrances against these grievances have been addressed without effect to that Government. Meantime in various parts of the Republic instances have been numerous of the murder, imprisonment, and plunder of our citizens by different parties claiming and exercising a local jurisdiction; but the central Government, although repeatedly urged thereto, have made no effort either to punish the authors of these outrages or to prevent their recurrence. No American citizen can now visit Mexico on lawful business without imminent danger to his person and property. There is no adequate protection to either, and in this respect our treaty with that Republic is almost a dead letter.

This state of affairs was brought to a crisis in May last by the promulgation of a decree levying a contribution pro rata upon all the capital in the Republic between certain specified amounts, whether held by Mexicans or foreigners. Mr. Forsyth, regarding this decree in the light of a "forced loan," formally protested against its application to his countrymen and advised them not to pay the contribution, but to suffer it to be forcibly exacted. Acting upon this advice, an American citizen refused to pay the contribution, and his property was seized by armed men to satisfy the amount. Not content with this, the Government proceeded still further and issued a decree banishing him from the country. Our minister immediately notified them that if this decree should be carried into execution he would feel it to be his duty to adopt "the most decided measures that belong to the powers and obligations of the representative office." Notwithstanding this warning, the banishment was enforced, and Mr. Forsyth promptly announced to the Government the suspension of the political relations of his legation with them until the pleasure of his own Government should be ascertained.

This Government did not regard the contribution imposed by the decree of the 15th May last to be in strictness a "forced loan," and as such prohibited by the tenth article of the treaty of 1826 between Great Britain and Mexico, to the benefits of which American citizens are entitled by treaty; yet the imposition of the contribution upon foreigners was considered an unjust and oppressive measure. Besides, internal factions in other parts of the Republic were at the same time levying similar exactions upon the property of our citizens and interrupting their commerce. There had been an entire failure on the part of our minister to secure redress for the wrongs which our citizens had endured, notwithstanding his persevering efforts. And from the temper manifested by the Mexican Government he had repeatedly assured us that no favorable change could be expected until the United States should "give striking evidence of their will and power to protect their citizens," and that "severe chastening is the only earthly remedy for our grievances." From this statement of facts it would have been worse than idle to direct Mr. Forsyth to retrace his steps and resume diplomatic relations with that Government, and it was therefore deemed proper to sanction his withdrawal of the legation from the City of Mexico.

Abundant cause now undoubtedly exists for a resort to hostilities against the Government still holding possession of the capital. Should they succeed in subduing the constitutional forces, all reasonable hope will then have expired of a peaceful settlement of our difficulties. On the other hand, should the constitutional party prevail and their authority be established over the Republic, there is reason to hope that they will be animated by a less unfriendly spirit and may grant that redress to American citizens which justice requires so far as they may possess the means. But for this expectation I should at once have recommended to Congress to grant the necessary power to the President to take possession of a sufficient portion of the remote and unsettled territory of Mexico, to be held in pledge until our injuries shall be redressed and our just demands be satisfied. We have already exhausted every milder means of obtaining justice. In such a case this remedy of reprisals is recognized by the law of nations, not only as just in itself, but as a means of preventing actual war.

But there is another view of our relations with Mexico, arising from the unhappy condition of affairs along our southwestern frontier, which demands immediate action. In that remote region, where there are but few white inhabitants, large bands of hostile and predatory Indians roam promiscuously over the Mexican States of Chihuahua and Sonora and our adjoining Territories. The local governments of these States are perfectly helpless and are kept in a state of constant alarm by the Indians. They have not the power, if they possessed the will, even to restrain lawless Mexicans from passing the border and committing depredations on our remote settlers. A state of anarchy and violence prevails throughout that distant frontier. The laws are a dead letter and life and property wholly insecure. For this reason the settlement of Arizona is arrested, whilst it is of great importance that a chain of inhabitants should extend all along its southern border sufficient for their own protection and that of the United States mail passing to and from California. Well-founded apprehensions are now entertained that the Indians and wandering Mexicans, equally lawless, may break up the important stage and postal communication recently established between our Atlantic and Pacific possessions. This passes very near to the Mexican boundary throughout the whole length of Arizona. I can imagine no possible remedy for these evils and no mode of restoring law and order on that remote and unsettled frontier but for the Government of the United States to assume a temporary protectorate over the northern portions of Chihuahua and Sonora and to establish military posts within the same; and this I earnestly recommend to Congress. This protection may be withdrawn as soon as local governments shall be established in these Mexican States capable of performing their duties to the United States, restraining the lawless, and preserving peace along the border.

I do not doubt that this measure will be viewed in a friendly spirit by the governments and people of Chihuahua and Sonora, as it will prove equally effectual for the protection of their citizens on that remote and lawless frontier as for citizens of the United States. And in this connection permit me to recall your attention to the condition of Arizona. The population of that Territory, numbering, as is alleged, more than 10,000 souls, are practically without a government, without laws, and without any regular administration of justice. Murder and other crimes are committed with impunity. This state of things calls loudly for redress, and I therefore repeat my recommendation for the establishment of a Territorial government over Arizona.

The political condition of the narrow isthmus of Central America, through which transit routes pass between the Atlantic and Pacific oceans, presents a subject of deep interest to all commercial nations. It is over these transits that a large proportion of the trade and travel between the European and Asiatic continents is destined to pass. To the United States these routes are of incalculable importance as a means of communication between their Atlantic and Pacific possessions. The latter now extend throughout seventeen degrees of latitude on the Pacific coast, embracing the important

State of California and the flourishing territories of Oregon and Washington. All commercial nations therefore have a deep and direct interest that these communications shall be rendered secure from interruption. If an arm of the sea connecting the two oceans penetrated through Nicaragua and Costa Rica, it could not be pretended that these States would have the right to arrest or retard its navigation to the injury of other nations. The transit by land over this narrow isthmus occupies nearly the same position. It is a highway in which they themselves have little interest when compared with the vast interests of the rest of the world. Whilst their rights of sovereignty ought to be respected, it is the duty of other nations to require that this important passage shall not be interrupted by the civil wars and revolutionary outbreaks which have so frequently occurred in that region. The stake is too important to be left at the mercy of rival companies claiming to hold conflicting contracts with Nicaragua. The commerce of other nations is not to stand still and await the adjustment of such petty controversies. The Government of the United States expect no more than this, and they will not be satisfied with less. They would not, if they could, derive any advantage from the Nicaragua transit not common to the rest of the World. Its neutrality and protection for the common use of all nations is their only object. They have no objection that Nicaragua shall demand and receive a fair compensation from the companies and individuals who may traverse the route, but they insist that it shall never hereafter be closed by an arbitrary decree of that Government. If disputes arise between it and those with whom they may have entered into contracts, these must be adjusted by some fair tribunal provided for the purpose, and the route must not be closed pending the controversy. This is our whole policy, and it can not fail to be acceptable to other nations.

All these difficulties might be avoided if, consistently with the good faith of Nicaragua, the use of this transit could be thrown open to general competition, providing at the same time for the payment of a reasonable rate to the Nicaraguan Government on passengers and freight. In August, 1852, the Accessory Transit Company made its first interoceanic trip over the Nicaraguan route, and continued in successful operation, with great advantage to the public, until the 18th February, 1856, when it was closed and the grant to this company as well as its charter were summarily and arbitrarily revoked by the Government of President Rivas. Previous to this date, however, in 1854, serious disputes concerning the settlement of their accounts had arisen between the company and the Government, threatening the interruption of the route at any moment. These the United States in vain endeavored to compose. It would be useless to narrate the various proceedings which took place between the parties up till the time when the transit was discontinued. Suffice it to say that since February, 1856, it has remained closed, greatly to the prejudice of citizens of the

United States. Since that time the competition has ceased between the rival routes of Panama and Nicaragua, and in consequence thereof an unjust and unreasonable amount has been exacted from our citizens for their passage to and from California

A treaty was signed on the 16th day of November, 1857, by the Secretary of State and minister of Nicaragua, under the stipulations of which the use and protection of the transit route would have been secured, not only to the United States, but equally to all other nations. How and on what pretext this treaty has failed to receive the ratification of the Nicaraguan Government will appear by the papers herewith communicated from the State Department. The principal objection seems to have been to the provision authorizing the United States to employ force to keep the route open in case Nicaragua should fail to perform her duty in this respect. From the feebleness of that Republic, its frequent changes of government, and its constant internal dissensions, this had become a most important stipulation, and one essentially necessary, not only for the security of the route, but for the safety of American citizens passing and repassing to and from our Pacific possessions. Were such a stipulation embraced in a treaty between the United States and Nicaragua, the knowledge of this fact would of itself most probably prevent hostile parties from committing aggressions on the route, and render our actual interference for its protection unnecessary.

The executive government of this country in its intercourse with foreign nations is limited to the employment of diplomacy alone. When this fails it can proceed no further. It can not legitimately resort to force without the direct authority of Congress, except in resisting and repelling hostile attacks. It would have no authority to enter the territories of Nicaragua even to prevent the destruction of the transit and protect the lives and property of our own citizens on their passage. It is true that on a sudden emergency of this character the President would direct any armed force in the vicinity to march to their relief, but in doing this he would act upon his own responsibility.

Under these circumstances I earnestly recommend to Congress the passage of an act authorizing the president, under such restrictions as they may deem proper, to employ the land and naval forces of the United States in preventing the transit from being obstructed or closed by lawless violence, and in protecting the lives and property of American citizens traveling thereupon, requiring at the same time that these forces shall be withdrawn the moment the danger shall have passed away. Without such a provision our citizens will be constantly exposed to interruption in their progress and to lawless violence.

A similar necessity exists for the passage of such an act for the protection of the Panama and Tehuantepec routes. In reference to the Panama route, the United States, by their existing treaty with New Granada, expressly guarantee the neutrality of the Isthmus, "with the view that the free transit from the one to the other sea may not be interrupted or embarrassed in any future time while this treaty exists."

In regard to the Tehuantepec route, which has been recently opened under the most favorable auspices, our treaty with Mexico of the 30th December, 1853, secures to the citizens of the United States a right of transit over it for their persons and merchandise and stipulates that neither Government shall "interpose any obstacle" thereto. It also concedes to the United States the "right to transport across the Isthmus, in closed bags, the mails of the United States not intended for distribution along the line of the communication; also the effects of the United States Government and its citizens which may be intended for transit and not for distribution on the Isthmus, free of custom-house or other charges by the Mexican Government."

These treaty stipulations with New Granada and Mexico, in addition to the considerations applicable to the Nicaragua route, seem to require legislation for the purpose of carrying them into effect.

The injuries which have been inflicted upon our citizens in Costa Rica and Nicaragua during the last two or three years have received the prompt attention of this Government. Some of these injuries were of the most aggravated character. The transaction at Virgin Bay in April, 1856, when a company of unarmed Americans, who were in no way connected with any belligerent conduct or party, were fired upon by the troops of Costa Rica and numbers of them killed and wounded, was brought to the knowledge of Congress by my predecessor soon after its occurrence, and was also presented to the Government of Costa Rica for that immediate investigation and redress which the nature of the case demanded. A similar course was pursued with reference to other outrages in these countries, some of which were hardly less aggravated in their character than the transaction at Virgin Bay. At the time, however, when our present minister to Nicaragua was appointed, in December, 1857, no redress had been obtained for any of these wrongs and no reply even had been received to the demands which had been made by this Government upon that of Costa Rica more than a year before. Our minister was instructed, therefore, to lose no time in expressing to those Governments the deep regret with which the President had witnessed this inattention to the just claims of the United States and in demanding their prompt and satisfactory adjustment. Unless this demand shall be complied with at an early day it will only remain for this Government to adopt such other measures as may be necessary in order to obtain for itself that justice which it has in vain attempted to secure by peaceful means from the Governments of Nicaragua and Costa Rica. While it has shown, and will continue to show, the most sincere regard for the rights and honor of these Republics, it can not permit this regard to be met by an utter neglect on their part of what is due to the Government and citizens of the United States.

Against New Granada we have long-standing causes of complaint, arising out of the unsatisfied claims of our citizens upon that Republic, and to these have been more recently added the outrages committed upon our citizens at Panama in April, 1856. A treaty for the adjustment of these difficulties was concluded by the Secretary of State and the minister of New Granada in September, 1857, which contained just and acceptable provisions for that purpose. This treaty was transmitted to Bogota and was ratified by the Government of New Granada, but with certain amendments. It was not, however, returned to this city until after the close of the last session of the Senate. It will be immediately transmitted to that body for their advice and consent, and should this be obtained it will remove all our existing causes of complaint against New Granada on the subject of claims.

Questions have arisen between the two Governments as to the right of New Granada to levy a tonnage duty upon the vessels of the United States in its ports of the Isthmus and to levy a passenger tax upon our citizens arriving in that country, whether with a design to remain there or to pass from ocean to ocean by the transit route; and also a tax upon the mail of the United States transported over the Panama Railroad. The Government of New Granada has been informed that the United States would consider the collection of either of these taxes as an act in violation of the treaty between the two countries, and as such would be resisted by the United States. At the same time, we are prepared to discuss these questions in a spirit of amity and justice and with a sincere desire to adjust them in a satisfactory manner. A negotiation for that purpose has already been commenced. No effort has recently been made to collect these taxes nor is any anticipated under present circumstances.

With the Empire of Brazil our relations are of the most friendly character. The productions of the two countries, and especially those of an agricultural nature, are such as to invite extensive mutual exchanges. A large quantity of American flour is consumed in Brazil, whilst more than treble the amount in value of Brazilian coffee is consumed in the United States. Whilst this is the case, a heavy duty has been levied until very recently upon the importation of American flour into Brazil. I am gratified, however, to be able to inform you that in September last this has been reduced from $1.32 to about 49 cents per barrel, and the duties on other articles of our production have been diminished in nearly the same proportion.

I regret to state that the Government of Brazil still continues to levy an export duty of about 11 per cent on coffee, notwithstanding this article is admitted free from duty in the United States. This is a heavy charge upon the consumers of coffee in our country, as we purchase half of the entire surplus crop of that article raised in Brazil. Our minister, under instructions, will reiterate his efforts to have this export duty removed, and it is hoped that the enlightened Government of the Emperor will adopt this wise, just, and equal policy. In that event, there is good reason to believe that the commerce between the two countries will greatly increase, much to the advantage of both. The claims of our citizens against the Government of Brazil are not in the aggregate of very large amount; but some of these rest upon plain principles of justice and their settlement ought not to be longer delayed. A renewed and earnest, and I trust a successful, effort will be made by our minister to procure their final adjustment.

On the 2d of June last Congress passed a joint resolution authorizing the President "to adopt such measures and use such force as in his judgment may be necessary and advisable" "for the the purpose of the differences between the United States and the Republic of Paraguay, in connection with the attack on the United States steamer Water Witch and with other measures referred to" in his annual message, and on the 12th of July following they made an appropriation to defray the expenses and compensation of a commissioner to that Republic should the President deem it proper to make such all appointment.

In compliance with these enactments, I have appointed a commissioner, who has proceeded to Paraguay with full powers and instructions to settle these differences in an amicable and peaceful manner if this be practicable. His experience and discretion justify the hope that he may prove successful in convincing the Paraguayan Government that it is due both to honor and justice that they should voluntarily and promptly make atonement for the wrongs which they have committed against the United States and indemnify our injured citizens whom they have forcibly despoiled of their property.

Should our commissioner prove unsuccessful after a sincere and earnest effort to accomplish the object of his mission, then no alternative will remain but the employment of force to obtain "just satisfaction" from Paraguay. In view of this contingency, the Secretary of the Navy, under my direction, has fitted out and dispatched a naval force to rendezvous near Buenos Ayres, which, it is believed, will prove sufficient for the occasion. It is my earnest desire, however, that it may not be found necessary to resort to this last alternative.

When Congress met in December last the business of the country had just been crushed by one of those periodical revulsions which are the inevitable consequence of our unsound and extravagant system of bank credits and inflated currency. With all the elements of national wealth in abundance, our manufactures were suspended, our useful public and private enterprises were arrested, and thousands of laborers were deprived of employment and reduced to want. Universal distress prevailed among the commercial, manufacturing, and mechanical classes. This revulsion was felt the more severely in the United States because similar causes had produced the like deplorable effects throughout the commercial nations of Europe. All were experiencing sad reverses at the same moment. Our manufacturers everywhere suffered severely, not because of the recent reduction in the tariff of duties on imports, but because there was no demand at any price for their productions. The people were obliged to restrict themselves in their purchases to articles of prime necessity. In the general prostration of business the iron manufacturers in different States probably suffered more than any other class, and much destitution was the inevitable consequence among the great number of workmen who had been employed in this useful branch of industry. There could be no supply where there was no demand. To present an example, there could be no demand for railroad iron after our magnificent system of railroads, extending its benefits to every portion of the Union, had been brought to a dead pause. The same consequences have resulted from similar causes to many other branches of useful manufactures. It is self-evident that where there is no ability to purchase manufactured articles these can not be sold, and consequently must cease to be produced.

No government, and especially a government of such limited powers as that of the United States, could have prevented the late revulsion. The whole commercial world seemed for years to have been rushing to this catastrophe. The same ruinous consequences would have followed in the United States whether the duties upon foreign imports had remained as they were under the tariff of 1846 or had been raised to a much higher standard. The tariff of 1857 had no agency in the result. The general causes existing throughout the world could not have been controlled by the legislation of any particular country.

The periodical revulsions which have existed in our past history must continue to return at intervals so long as our present unbounded system of bank credits shall prevail. They will, however, probably be the less severe in future, because it is not to be expected, at least for many years to come, that the commercial nations of Europe, with whose interests our own are so materially involved, will expose themselves to similar calamities. But this subject was treated so much at large in my last annual message that I shall not now pursue it further. Still, I respectfully renew the recommendation in favor of the passage of a uniform bankrupt law applicable to banking institutions. This is all the direct power over the subject which I believe the Federal Government possesses. Such a law would mitigate, though it might not prevent, the evil. The instinct of self-preservation might produce a wholesome restraint upon their banking business if they knew in advance that a suspension of specie payments would inevitably produce their civil death.

But the effects of the revulsion are now slowly but surely passing away. The energy and enterprise of our citizens, with our unbounded resources, will within the period of another year restore a state of wholesome industry and trade. Capital has again accumulated in our large cities. The rate of interest is there very low. Confidence is gradually reviving, and so soon as it is discovered that this capital can be profitably employed in commercial and manufacturing enterprises and in the construction of railroads and other works of public and private improvement prosperity will again smile throughout the land. It is vain, however, to disguise the fact from ourselves that a speculative inflation of our currency without a corresponding inflation in other countries whose manufactures come into competition with our own must ever produce disastrous results to our domestic manufactures. No tariff short of absolute prohibition can prevent these evil consequences. In connection with this subject it is proper to refer to our financial condition. The same causes which have produced pecuniary distress throughout the country have so reduced the amount of imports from foreign countries that the revenue has proved inadequate to meet the necessary expenses of the Government. To supply the deficiency, Congress, by the act of December 23, 1857, authorized the issue of $20,000,000 of Treasury notes; and this proving inadequate, they authorized, by the act of June 14, 1858, a loan of $20,000,000," to be applied to the payment of appropriations made by law."

No statesman would advise that we should go on increasing the national debt to meet the ordinary expenses of the Government. This would be a most ruinous policy. In case of war our credit must be our chief resource, at least for the first year, and this would be greatly impaired by having contracted a large debt in time of peace. It is our true policy to increase our revenue so as to equal our expenditures. It would be ruinous to continue to borrow. Besides, it may be proper to observe that the incidental protection thus afforded by a revenue tariff would at the present moment to some extent increase the confidence of the manufacturing interests and give a fresh impulse to our reviving business. To this surely no person will object.

In regard to the mode of assessing and collecting duties under a strictly revenue tariff, I have long entertained and often expressed the opinion that sound policy requires this should be done by specific duties in cases to which these can be properly applied. They are well adapted to commodities which are usually sold by weight or by measure, and which from their nature are of equal or of nearly equal value. Such, for example, are the articles of iron of different classes, raw sugar, and foreign wines and spirits.

In my deliberate judgment specific duties are the best, if not the only, means of securing the revenue against false and fraudulent invoices, and such has been the practice adopted for this purpose by other commercial nations. Besides, specific duties would afford to the American manufacturer the incidental advantages to which he is fairly entitled under a revenue tariff. The present system is a sliding scale to his disadvantage. Under it, when prices are high and business prosperous, the duties rise in amount when he least requires their aid. On the contrary, when prices fall and he is struggling against adversity, the duties are diminished in the same proportion, greatly to his injury. Neither would there be danger that a higher rate of duty than that intended by Congress could be levied in the form of specific duties. It would be easy to ascertain the average value of any imported article for a series of years, and, instead of subjecting it to an ad valorem duty at a certain rate per centum, to substitute in its place an equivalent specific duty.

By such an arrangement the consumer would not be injured. It is true he might have to pay a little more duty on a given article in one year, but, if so, he would pay a little less in another, and in a series of years these would counterbalance each other and amount to the same thing so far as his interest is concerned. This inconvenience would be trifling when contrasted with the additional security thus afforded against frauds upon the revenue, in which every consumer is directly interested.

I have thrown out these suggestions as the fruit of my own observation, to which Congress, in their better judgment, will give such weight as they may justly deserve.

The report of the Secretary of the Treasury will explain in detail the operations of that Department of the Government. The receipts into the Treasury from all sources during the fiscal year ending June 30, 1858, including the Treasury notes authorized by the act of December 23, 1857, were $70,273,869.59, which amount, with the balance of $17,710,114.27 remaining in the Treasury at the commencement of the year, made an aggregate for the service of the year of $87,983,983.86.

The public expenditures during the fiscal year ending June 30, 1858, amounted to $81,585,667.76, of which $9,684,537.99 were applied to the payment of the public debt and the redemption of Treasury notes with the interest thereon, leaving in the Treasury on July 1, 1858, being the commencement of the present fiscal year, $6,398,316.10.

The receipts into the Treasury during the first quarter of the present fiscal year, commencing the 1st of July, 1858, including one-half of the loan of $20,000,000, with the premium upon it, authorized by the act of June 14, 1858, were $25,230,879.46, and the estimated receipts for the remaining three quarters to the 30th of June, 1859, from ordinary sources are $38,500,000, making, with the balance before stated, an aggregate of $70,129,195.56.

The expenditures during the first quarter of the present fiscal year were $21,708,198.51, of which $1,010,142.37 were applied to the payment of the public debt and the redemption of Treasury notes and the interest thereon. The estimated expenditures during the remaining three quarters to June 30,

1859, are $52,357,698.48, making an aggregate of $74,065,896.99, being an excess of expenditure beyond the estimated receipts into the Treasury from ordinary sources during the fiscal year to the 30th of June, 1859, of $3,936,701.43. Extraordinary means are placed by law within the command of the Secretary of the Treasury, by the reissue of Treasury notes redeemed and by negotiating the balance of the loan authorized by the act of June 14, 1858, to the extent of $11,000,000, which, if realized during the present fiscal year, will leave a balance in the Treasury on the 1st day of July, 1859, of $7,063,298.57.

The estimated receipts during the next fiscal year, ending June 30, 1860, are $62,000,000, which, with the above-estimated balance of $7,063,298.57 make an aggregate for the service of the next fiscal year of $69,063,298.57. The estimated expenditures during the next fiscal year, ending June 30, 1860, are $73,139,147.46, which leaves a deficit of estimated means, compared with the estimated expenditures, for that year, commencing on July 1, 1859, of $4,075,848.89.

In addition to this sum the Postmaster-General will require from the Treasury for the service of the Post-Office Department $3,838,728, as explained in the report of the Secretary of the Treasury, which will increase the estimated deficit on June 30, 1860, to $7,914,576.89. To provide for the payment of this estimated deficiency, which will be increased by such appropriations as may be made by Congress not estimated for in the report of the Treasury Department, as well as to provide for the gradual redemption from year to year of the outstanding Treasury notes, the Secretary of the Treasury recommends such a revision of the present tariff as will raise the required amount. After what I have already said I need scarcely add that I concur in the opinion expressed in his report-that the public debt should not be increased by an additional loan-and would therefore strongly urge upon Congress the duty of making at their present session the necessary provision for meeting these liabilities.

The public debt on July 1, 1858, the commencement of the present fiscal year, was $25,155,977.66.

During the first quarter of the present year the sum of $10,000,000 has been negotiated of the loan authorized by the act of June 14, 1858, making the present outstanding public debt, exclusive of Treasury notes, $35,155,977.66. There was on the 1st of July, 1858, of Treasury notes issued by authority of the act of December 23, 1857, unredeemed, the sum of $19,754,800, making the amount of actual indebtedness at that date $54,910,777.66. To this will be added $10,000,000 during the present fiscal year, this being the remaining half of the loan of $20,000,000 not yet negotiated.

The rapid increase of the public debt and the necessity which exists for a modification of the tariff to meet even the ordinary expenses of the

Government ought to admonish us all, in our respective spheres of duty, to the practice of rigid economy. The objects of expenditure should be limited in number, as far as this may be practicable, and the appropriations necessary to carry them into effect ought to be disbursed under the strictest accountability. Enlightened economy does not consist in the refusal to appropriate money for constitutional purposes essential to the defense, progress, and prosperity of the Republic, but in taking care that none of this money shall be wasted by mismanagement in its application to the objects designated by law.

Comparisons between the annual expenditure at the present time and what it was ten or twenty years ago are altogether fallacious. The rapid increase of our country in extent and population renders a corresponding increase of expenditure to some extent unavoidable. This is constantly creating new objects of expenditure and augmenting the amount required for the old. The true questions, then, are, Have these objects been unnecessarily multiplied, or has the amount expended upon any or all of them been larger than comports with due economy? In accordance with these principles, the heads of the different Executive Departments of the Government have been instructed to reduce their estimates for the next fiscal year to the lowest standard consistent with the efficiency of the service, and this duty they have performed in a spirit of just economy. The estimates of the Treasury, War, Navy, and Interior Departments have each been in some degree reduced, and unless a sudden and unforeseen emergency should arise it is not anticipated that a deficiency will exist in either within the present or the next fiscal year. The Post-Office Department is placed in a peculiar position, different from the other Departments, and to this I shall hereafter refer.

I invite Congress to institute a rigid scrutiny to ascertain whether the expenses in all the Departments can not be still further reduced, and I promise them all the aid in my power in pursuing the investigation.

I transmit herewith the reports made to me by the Secretaries of War, of the Navy, of the Interior, and of the Postmaster-General. They each contain valuable information and important recommendations, to which I invite the attention of Congress.

In my last annual message I took occasion to recommend the immediate construction of ten small steamers of light draft, for the purpose of increasing the efficiency of the Navy. Congress responded to the recommendation by authorizing the construction of eight of them. The progress which has been made in executing this authority is stated in the report of the Secretary of the Navy. I concur with him in the opinion that a greater number of this class of vessels is necessary for the purpose of protecting in a more efficient manner the persons and property of American citizens on the high seas and in foreign countries, as well as in guarding more effectually our own coasts. I accordingly recommend the passage of an act for this purpose.

The suggestions contained in the report of the Secretary of the Interior, especially those in regard to the disposition of the public domain, the pension and bounty-land system, the policy toward the Indians, and the amendment of our patent laws, are worthy of the serious consideration of Congress.

The Post-Office Department occupies a position very different from that of the other Departments. For many years it was the policy of the Government to render this a self-sustaining Department; and if this can not now be accomplished, in the present condition of the country, we ought to make as near an approach to it as may be practicable.

The Postmaster-General is placed in a most embarrassing position by the existing laws. He is obliged to carry these into effect. He has no other alternative. He finds, however, that this can not be done without heavy demands upon the Treasury over and above what is received for postage, and these have been progressively increasing from year to year until they amounted for the last fiscal year, ending on the 30th of June, 1858, to more than $4,500,000, whilst it is estimated that for the present fiscal year they will amount to $6,290,000. These sums are exclusive of the annual appropriation of $700,000 for "compensation for the mail service performed for the two Houses of Congress and the other Departments and officers of the Government in the transmission of free matter."

The cause of these large deficits is mainly attributable to the increased expense of transporting the mails. In 1852 the sum paid for this service was but a fraction above four millions and a quarter. Since that year it has annually increased, until in 1858 it has reached more than eight millions and a quarter, and for the service of 1859 it is estimated that it will amount to more than $10,000,000.

The receipts of the Post-Office Department can be made to approach or to equal its expenditure only by means of the legislation of Congress. In applying any remedy care should be taken that the people shall not be deprived of the advantages which they are fairly entitled to enjoy from the Post-Office Department. The principal remedies recommended to the consideration of Congress by the Postmaster-General are to restore the former rate of postage upon single letters to 5 cents; to substitute for the franking privilege the delivery to those now entitled to enjoy it of post-office stamps for their correspondence, and to direct the Department in making contracts for the transportation of the mail to confine itself to the payment of the sum necessary for this single purpose, without requiring it to be transported in post coaches or carriages of any particular description. Under the present system the expense to the Government is greatly increased by requiring that the mail shall be carried in such vehicles as will accommodate passengers. This will be done, without pay from the Department, over all roads where the travel will remunerate the contractors. These recommendations deserve the grave consideration of Congress. I would again call your attention to the construction of a Pacific railroad. Time and reflection have but served to confirm me in the truth and justice of the observations which I made on this subject in my last annual message, to which I beg leave respectfully to refer.

It is freely admitted that it would be inexpedient for this Government to exercise the power of constructing the Pacific railroad by its own immediate agents. Such a policy would increase the patronage of the Executive to a dangerous extent, and introduce a system of jobbing and corruption which no vigilance on the part of Federal officials could either prevent or detect. This can only be done by the keen eye and active and careful supervision of individual and private interest. The construction of this road ought therefore to be committed to companies incorporated by the States or other agencies whose pecuniary interests would be directly involved. Congress might then assist them in the work by grants of land or of money, or both, under such conditions and restrictions as would secure the transportation of troops and munitions of war free from any charge and that of the United States mail at a fair and reasonable price.

The progress of events since the commencement of your last session has shown how soon difficulties disappear before a firm and determined resolution. At that time such a road was deemed by wise and patriotic men to be a visionary project. The great distance to be overcome and the intervening mountains and deserts in the way were obstacles which, in the opinion of many, could not be surmounted. Now, after the lapse of but a single year, these obstacles, it has been discovered, are far less formidable than they were supposed to be, and mail stages with passengers now pass and repass regularly twice in each week, by a common wagon road, between San Francisco and St. Louis and Memphis in less than twenty-five days. The service has been as regularly performed as it was in former years between New York and this city.

Whilst disclaiming all authority to appropriate money for the construction of this road, except that derived from the war-making power of the Constitution, there are important collateral considerations urging us to undertake the work as speedily as possible. The first and most momentous of these is that such a road would be a powerful bond of union between the States east and west of the Rocky Mountains. This is so self-evident as to require no illustration.

But again, in a commercial point of view, I consider this the great question of the day. With the eastern front of our Republic stretching along the Atlantic and its western front along the Pacific, if all the parts should be united by a safe, easy, and rapid intercommunication we must necessarily command a very large proportion of the trade both of Europe and Asia. Our recent treaties with China and Japan will open these rich and populous Empires to our commerce; and the history of the world proves that the nation which has gained possession of the trade with eastern Asia has always become wealthy and powerful. The peculiar geographical position of California and our Pacific possessions invites American capital and enterprise into this fruitful field. To reap the rich harvest, however, it is an indispensable prerequisite that we shall first have a railroad to convey and circulate its products throughout every portion of the Union. Besides, such a railroad through our temperate latitude, which would not be impeded by the frosts and snows of winter nor by the tropical heats of summer, would attract to itself much of the travel and the trade of all nations passing between Europe and Asia.

On the 21st of August last Lieutenant J. N. Maffit, of the United States brig Dolphin, captured the slaver Echo (formerly the Putnam, of New Orleans) near Kay Verde, on the coast of Cuba, with more than 300 African negroes on board. The prize, under the command of Lieutenant Bradford, of the United States Navy, arrived at Charleston on the 27th August, when the negroes, 306 in number, were delivered into the custody of the United States marshal for the district of South Carolina. They were first placed in Castle Pinckney, and afterwards in Fort Sumter, for safe-keeping, and were detained there until the 19th September, when the survivors, 271 in number, were delivered on board the United States steamer Niagara to be transported to the coast of Africa under the charge of the agent of the United States, pursuant to the provisions of the act of the 3d March, 1819, "in addition to the acts prohibiting the slave trade." Under the second section of this act the President is "authorized to make such regulations and arrangements as he may deem expedient for the safe-keeping, support, and removal beyond the limits of the United States of all such negroes, mulattoes, or persons of color" captured by vessels of the United States as may be delivered to the marshal of the district into which they are brought, "and to appoint a proper person or persons residing upon the coast of Africa as agent or agents for receiving the negroes, mulattoes, or persons of color delivered from on board vessels seized in the prosecution of the slave trade by commanders of United States armed vessels."

A doubt immediately arose as to the true construction of this act. It is quite clear from its terms that the President was authorized to provide "for the safe-keeping, support, and removal" of these negroes up till the time of their delivery to the agent on the coast of Africa, but no express provision was made for their protection and support after they had reached the place of their destination. Still, an agent was to be pointed to receive them in Africa, and it could not have been supposed that Congress intended he should desert them at the moment they were received and turn them loose on that inhospitable coast to perish for want of food or to become again the victims of the slave trade. Had this been the intention of Congress, the employment of an agent to receive them, who is required to reside on the coast, was unnecessary, and they might have been landed by our vessels anywhere in Africa and left exposed to the sufferings and the fate which would certainly await them.

Mr. Monroe, in his special message of December 17, 1819, at the first session after the act was passed, announced to Congress what in his opinion was its true construction. He believed it to be his duty under it to follow these unfortunates into Africa and make provision for them there until they should be able to provide for themselves. In communicating this interpretation of the act to Congress he stated that some doubt had been entertained as to its true intent and meaning, and he submitted the question to them so that they might, "should it be deemed advisable, amend the same before further proceedings are had under it." Nothing was done by Congress to explain the act, and Mr. Monroe proceeded to carry it into execution according to his own interpretation. This, then, became the practical construction. When the Africans from on board the Echo were delivered to the marshal at Charleston, it became my duty to consider what disposition ought to be made of them under the law. For many reasons it was expedient to remove them from that locality as speedily as possible. Although the conduct of the authorities and citizens of Charleston in giving countenance to the execution of the law was just what might have been expected from their high character, yet a prolonged continuance of 300 Africans in the immediate vicinity of that city could not have failed to become a source of inconvenience and anxiety to its inhabitants. Where to send them was the question. There was no portion of the coast of Africa to which they could be removed with any regard to humanity except to Liberia. Under these circumstances an agreement was entered into with the Colonization Society on the 7th of September last, a copy of which is herewith transmitted, under which the society engaged, for the consideration of $45,000, to receive these Africans in Liberia from the agent of the United States and furnish them during the period of one year thereafter with comfortable shelter, clothing, provisions, and medical attendance, causing the children to receive schooling, and all, whether children or adults, to be instructed in the arts of civilized life suitable to their condition. This aggregate of $45,000 was based upon an allowance of $150 for each individual; and as there has been considerable mortality among them and may be more before they reach Africa, the society have agreed, in an equitable spirit, to make such a deduction from the amount as under the circumstances may appear just and reasonable. This can not be fixed until we shall ascertain the actual number which may become a charge to the society. It was also distinctly agreed that under no circumstances shall this Government be called upon for any additional expenses. The agents of the society manifested a laudable desire to conform to the wishes of the Government throughout the transaction. They assured me that after a careful calculation they would be required to expend the sum of $150 on each individual in complying with the agreement, and they would have nothing left to remunerate them for their care, trouble, and responsibility. At all events, I could make no better arrangement, and there was no other alternative. During the period when the Government itself, through its own agents, undertook the task of providing for captured negroes in Africa the cost per head was very much greater.

There having been no outstanding appropriation applicable to this purpose, I could not advance any money on the agreement. I therefore recommend that an appropriation may be made of the amount necessary to carry it into effect.

Other captures of a similar character may, and probably will, be made by our naval forces, and I earnestly recommend that Congress may amend the second section of the act of March 3, 1819, so as to free its construction from the ambiguity which has so long existed and render the duty of the President plain in executing its provisions.

I recommend to your favorable regard the local interests of the District of Columbia. As the residence of Congress and the Executive Departments of the Government, we can not fail to feel a deep concern in its welfare. This is heightened by the high character and the peaceful and orderly conduct of its resident inhabitants.

I can not conclude without performing the agreeable duty of expressing my gratification that Congress so kindly responded to the recommendation of my last annual message by affording me sufficient time before the close of their late session for the examination of all the bills presented to me for approval. This change in the practice of Congress has proved to be a wholesome reform. It exerted a beneficial influence on the transaction of legislative business and elicited the general approbation of the country. It enabled Congress to adjourn with that dignity and deliberation so becoming to the representatives of this great Republic, without having crowded into general appropriation bills provisions foreign to their nature and of doubtful constitutionality and expediency. Let me warmly and strongly commend this precedent established by themselves as a guide to their proceedings during the present session.

JAMES BUCHANAN

www.ingramcontent.com/pod-product-compliance
Lightning Source LLC
Chambersburg PA
CBHW070513290526
45790CB00003B/1217